D0264719

To nathaniel

Merry Christmas

Love

Auntie Kirsty +
Chloe
X   X

Disney·PIXAR

STORY COLLECTION

Parragon

Bath · New York · Singapore · Hong Kong · Cologne · Delhi · Melbourne

TABLE OF CONTENTS

"The Supers Save the Day" adapted from The Incredibles Amazing 3-D Adventure written by Elle D. Risco and illustrated by the Disney Storybook Artists. Copyright © 2004 Disney Enterprises, Inc./Pixar. Based on the movie The Incredibles. Copyright © 2004 Disney Enterprises, Inc./Pixar. The term OMNIDROID used by permission of Lucasfilm Ltd.

"A Tight Squeeze" adapted from the original story "A Tight Squeeze" from Disney•Pixar 5-Minute Stories written by Laura Driscoll and illustrated by Ken Becker and the Disney Storybook Artists. Copyright © 2005 Disney Enterprises, Inc. Based on the characters from the movies Toy Story Copyright © 1995 Disney Enterprises, Inc. and Toy Story 2 Copyright © 1999 Disney Enterprises, Inc./Pixar. Original Toy Story elements © Disney Enterprises, Inc. Etch A Sketch® © The Ohio Art Company. Slinky® Dog © James Industries.

"Bedtime for Billy" adapted from the original book Monsters Get Scared of the Dark, Too written by Melissa Lagonegro, illustrated by Atelier Philippe Harchy, and originally published by Random House. © 2003 Disney Enterprises, Inc./Pixar. Based on the characters from the movie Monsters, Inc. Copyright © 2001 Disney Enterprises, Inc./Pixar.

"Nemo and the Tank Gang" adapted by Amy Edgar is based on the movie Finding Nemo. Copyright © 2003 Disney Enterprises, Inc./Pixar.

"A Super Summer Barbecue" written by Amy Edgar is based on the characters from the movie The Incredibles. Copyright © 2004 Disney Enterprises, Inc./Pixar.

"Super Annoying!" adapted from the original story "Super Annoying!" from Disney•Pixar 5-Minute Stories written by Laura Driscoll and illustrated by Ken Becker and the Disney Storybook Artists. Copyright © 2005 Disney Enterprises, Inc./Pixar. Based on the characters from the movie The Incredibles. Copyright © 2004 Disney Enterprises, Inc./Pixar.

"Mike's Dog Problem" adapted from the original book Monsters Get Scared of Dogs, Too written by Melissa Lagonegro, illustrated by Atelier Philippe Harchy, and originally published by Random House. © 2004 Disney Enterprises, Inc./Pixar. Based on the characters from the movie Monsters, Inc. Copyright © 2001 Disney Enterprises, Inc./Pixar.

"Race Day" adapted by Paula Richards are based on the movie Cars. "Red's Tune-Up Blues" written by Paula Richards is based on the characters from the movie Cars. Copyright © 2006 Disney Enterprises, Inc./Pixar. Disney/Pixar elements © Disney/Pixar; Hudson Hornet is a trademark of DaimlerChrysler Corporation; Volkswagen trademarks, design patents and copyrights are used with the approval of the owner, Volkswagen AG; Model T is a registered trademark of Ford Motor Company; Fiat is a trademark of Fiat S.p.A.; Mack is a registered trademark of Mack Trucks, Inc.; Chevrolet Impala is a trademark of General Motors; Porsche is a trademark of Porsche; Jeep® and the Jeep® grille design are registered trademarks of DaimlerChrysler Corporation; Mercury is a registered trademark of Ford Motor Company; Plymouth Superbird is a trademark of DaimlerChrysler Corporation; Cadillac Coup de Ville is a trademark of General Motors. Petty marks used by permission of Petty Marketing LLC. Cadillac Ranch background inspired by the Cadillac Ranch by Ant Farm (Lord, Michels and Marquez) © 1974.

"Buzz to the Rescue!" adapted from the original story "Buzz to the Rescue!" from Disney's 5-Minute Adventure Stories written by Sarah Heller. Copyright © 2002 Disney Enterprises, Inc./Pixar. Based on the characters from the movies Toy Story Copyright © 1995 Disney Enterprises, Inc. and Toy Story 2 Copyright © 1999 Disney Enterprises, Inc./Pixar. Original Toy Story elements © Disney Enterprises, Inc. Etch A Sketch® © The Ohio Art Company. Slinky® Dog © James Industries.

Unless otherwise noted, all illustrations by the Disney Storybook Artists.

First published by Parragon in 2007
Parragon
Queen Street House
4 Queen Street
Bath BA1 1HE, UK

Copyright © 2007 Disney Enterprises, Inc. / Pixar
All rights reserved. No part of this publication may be reproduced, stored in a retrieval system or transmitted, in any form or by any means, electronic, mechanical, photocopying, recording or otherwise, without the prior permission of the copyright holder.

ISBN 978-1-4054-9834-0

Printed in China

Disney PRESENTS A PIXAR FILM

THE INCREDIBLES

THE SUPERS SAVE THE DAY

In the city of Municiburg, everyone slept soundly at night. That's because they knew that the Supers, a group of heroes with special powers, would keep them safe.

One night, Mr Incredible, a Super who was incredibly strong, was on his way to his wedding when he heard about a robbery that was in progress. He tried to stop the thief. While he was there, a boy named Buddy flew in using some rocket boots that he'd made.

He didn't have any powers, but he was determined to become Mr Incredible's sidekick.

But the Super didn't want a sidekick. "I work alone," he said. "Go home."

Buddy didn't listen. He tried to show how helpful he could be and the bank robber got away. Mr Incredible was upset and made it very clear he didn't want Buddy's help ever again.

Then Mr Incredible went to the church. He was getting married to Elastigirl, a Super who could stretch her body into all kinds of shapes. He was very late, but she forgave him and they married in front of their Super friends. They were very happy together.

One day, Mr Incredible saved someone who didn't want to be saved. He was sued and it wasn't long before the rest of the Supers were sued for their good deeds, too. The government decided the lawsuits were too expensive. So, they put all of the heroes in the Super Relocation Programme and gave them new names and regular jobs. The only condition was that they couldn't use their powers. That way no one would ever find out who they really were – and no one could sue them.

11

Mr Incredible and Elastigirl became Bob and Helen Parr.
They lived in the suburbs and had a house and three children:
Violet, Dash and Jack-Jack. They tried to live a normal life,
but sometimes things got a little crazy around the house. After
all, Violet could generate force fields and turn invisible and
Dash had Super speed. Little Jack-Jack didn't seem to have
any powers yet.

Bob worked at an insurance company, but he missed his old life. One night, he and his friend Lucius, who'd been a Super called Frozone, used their powers to save some people from a fire. Unfortunately, they didn't realize that someone was watching them from the shadows. . . .

Before long, the person who'd seen them contacted Bob. Her name was Mirage and she knew that he'd been a Super. She had a top secret job for him. Bob decided to take it. After all, he missed doing Super work.

Bob put on his old Super suit and told Helen that he was going on a business trip. Then he got on a plane with Mirage and they flew to an island. She told him it was a government testing facility and that they'd lost control of an experimental robot called the Omnidroid.

"It's a learning robot," she told him. "Every moment you spend fighting it only increases its knowledge of how to beat you."

Mr Incredible used all of his strength against the Omnidroid. He was finally able to trick it into defeating itself.

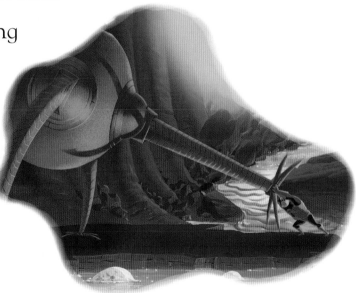

When Mr Incredible went home, he felt like a new man. He started to work out and got his old friend Edna Mode to design him a new-and-improved Super suit.

Soon, Bob got another call from Mirage about more work on the island and he eagerly agreed to go. But when he got there, he realized that he'd been set up. It turned out that Mirage's boss was

Buddy, the same boy who'd wanted to be Mr Incredible's sidekick long ago. But he wasn't a boy any longer. He'd grown up and now he called himself Syndrome. He was still bitter about how Mr Incredible had treated him.

"All I wanted was to help you!" Syndrome cried. He'd invented the Omnidroid and had an evil plan to use it to become more powerful. He tried to capture Mr Incredible, but the Super escaped. Later, he snuck back into Syndrome's headquarters to learn more about the villain's scheme. It wasn't long before Syndrome found him and trapped him with giant blobs of goo.

Meanwhile, back at home, Helen began to suspect that Bob was up to something. She went to visit Edna Mode, who explained that she'd just made Bob a new Super suit. In fact, she'd designed suits for the whole family!

"Each suit contains a homing device," the designer explained.

Helen left the children with a babysitter and activated the device. Then she put on her Super suit and borrowed a jet. As she flew towards the homing signal, she discovered that Dash and Violet had stowed away with her.

Just then, a missile hit the plane. Syndrome had seen them! The plane went down and Elastigirl and the children landed in the ocean. Elastigirl turned herself into the shape of a boat and Dash used his Super speed to power them through the water.

When they got to shore, Elastigirl left the children in a cave and told them to stay put. Then she went to find her husband.

While Helen was gone, Syndrome launched a rocket. Its exhaust travelled through the cave that Violet and Dash were in. The children escaped just in time and ended up in a jungle. Soon, they set off one of Syndrome's alarms.

It wasn't long before guards came after them. "Dash, run!" Violet yelled. She turned herself invisible and hurried away.

Dash took off in a blur of motion. This was the first time he'd ever used his powers against bad guys. The guards went after him in flying ships called velocipods. Dash grabbed a vine and swung on it, but it snapped. "*Aaaaah!*" he screamed as he fell. He hit the top of a velocipod. He punched the guard, then jumped off just before it hit a cliff. Then he zoomed across the top of the ocean and back to the jungle, where he ran into Violet.

She put a force field around them and together they fought the guards as best as they could.

Inside Syndrome's headquarters, Elastigirl had located her husband. Mirage had just released him from his prison cell. Mirage had finally realized just how evil Syndrome really was. She warned Mr Incredible and his wife that their children had set off the security alarms.

Mr Incredible and Elastigirl raced to the jungle to save their children. When they got there, they saw that Violet and Dash were using their powers on the guards – and holding their own!

Mr Incredible and Elastigirl joined in the fight. The family was winning – until Syndrome showed up. The villain used an immobi-ray on them so that they couldn't move. Then he trapped them in high-tech suspension beams and flew off to the city of Metroville – where the Omnidroid was already wreaking havoc.

Syndrome planned to prove to everyone that he was a hero by showing up and defeating the robot. No one would ever know that he'd made the robot. He would become a bigger hero than Mr Incredible ever had been.

Luckily, Violet was able to use a force field to break the immobi-ray's hold on her. She freed the rest of her family and they flew to the city in a van that was attached to a rocket.

When they arrived, the Omnidroid was completely out of control, destroying everything in sight. Syndrome tried to use a remote control to stop it, but it even knocked *him* out.

It was up to the Supers to save the day. Individually, they were awesome, but as a team, they were unstoppable! Their

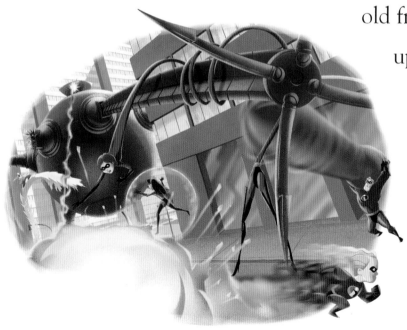

old friend, Frozone, showed up and together they defeated the Omnidroid. The people of the city cheered, glad that the Supers had returned.

24

When the Incredibles got home, Syndrome was there. He'd just taken Jack-Jack and was flying above their house. All of a sudden, the baby turned himself into a mini-monster. The villain dropped him in shock. But Jack-Jack wasn't done yet. He ripped a valve off of Syndrome's rocket boots. The villain plummeted to the ground, he was gone forever. Luckily, Jack-Jack ended up safe in his mother's arms.

The Incredibles went back to their normal lives. But they were ready to use their powers to keep the world safe again . . . as a family.

Disney · PIXAR

TOY STORY AND BEYOND!

A Tight Squeeze

"Calling all toys, calling all toys," Woody the cowboy announced. "The coast is clear."

It was early one morning and Andy had just left for school. Since he would be gone all day, the toys had the room to themselves. They were ready to have some fun.

"So, Woody," Rex the dinosaur said as the toys gathered in the centre of the floor, "what's this game you were telling us about?"

Woody smiled. "It's called 'sardines,'" he replied. "It's like hide-and-seek, except the toy who's 'It' is the one who hides, and everyone else tries to find him or her."

Buzz Lightyear, the space ranger, scratched his head. "I'm not sure I understand," he said. "What do you do when you find the hider?"

"Yeah, what do you do next?" asked Slinky Dog.

"Well," said Woody, "that's the fun part. When you find the hider, you hide with them and wait for someone else to find you both. Then, the next toy to find you hides with you too, and so on and so on. Get it?"

Most of the toys smiled and nodded at Woody. Bo Peep giggled. "Ooh, this is going to be fun!" she cried.

But Jessie the cowgirl was still confused about one thing. "So, by the end of the game, everyone is hiding together in one spot?" she asked.

Woody nodded. "Right," he said, "except for the last toy, who is still looking for the hiders. In the next game, that toy is 'It' - the one who hides!"

Now all of the toys understood the rules and were ready to play!

"So let's decide who's 'It,'" Woody suggested. "I'm thinking of a number between one and one hundred. Whoever guesses closest to that number is 'It.'"

The toys took turns guessing. Woody was thinking of forty-nine. Hamm the piggy bank guessed forty-seven. He was the closest, so he was 'It.'

"Okay, everybody," Woody announced. "Close your eyes and count to twenty-five while Hamm hides."

The toys covered their eyes and began to count aloud, "One . . . two . . . three . . ."

Meanwhile, Hamm hurried away and started to look for a good hiding place. "Hmm . . ." he said to himself as he considered hiding inside Andy's toy chest. "Nah, too obvious. That's the first place they'd look."

"Ten . . . eleven . . . twelve . . ." the toys continued counting.

Hamm hurried over to Andy's bed and peeked under the dust ruffle. It was dark and dusty under the bed. "Nah," said Hamm. "Too scary. I'm not hiding under there all by myself."

"Eighteen . . . nineteen . . . twenty . . ." the toys counted off.

Hamm was running out of time! With only seconds to spare, he spotted one of Andy's old lunch boxes, raced over to it, hopped inside and closed the lid.

"Whew!" he whispered to himself. "That was close, but I'm hidden!" Only then did Hamm realize that it was even darker inside the closed lunch box than it was under Andy's bed. "Huh," he said, feeling slightly panicked but trying to keep his cool. "I, uh, wonder how long it'll take for someone to find me?"

The next toy to open the lunch box lid was Woody, whose eyes lit up when he saw Hamm inside. He glanced over his shoulder to make sure he wasn't being watched before he hopped inside the lunch box.

Soon, the lid opened and Jessie peeked in. "Yippee!" she cried. "Found ya, didn't I?"

But there wasn't much space left, so she got wedged between Hamm and Woody.

"Well, gosh, boys," said Jessie. "It's a little bit crowded in here, isn't it?"

A minute later, the lunch box lid was lifted open and a Green Army Man peeked in. Upon spotting the toys, he waved to his battalion. "Target located. Move, move, move!" he ordered. The Green Army Men scaled the outside of the lunch box and rappelled down the inside.

Within seconds, they were all in and the lid was closed again.

Woody started to feel a little cramped. "Uh, Hamm," he said, "could you scooch over a little?"

"Gee, Woody," Hamm replied, "I'd like to help you out, but I'm already squished up against the sergeant here." He pointed to the Green Army Man on the other side of him.

"Hmm . . ." said Woody. "This may become a problem."

The situation got worse as more and more toys found the hiders. Slinky Dog only managed to fit inside by standing over a Green Army Man.

"Ow, your paw is in my ear," the Green Army Man told Slinky Dog.

"Sorry, there's nowhere else for me to put it," Slinky Dog said.

Buzz heard the toys complaining and located the hiding place. "Make way, folks!" he exclaimed as he piled in. But as hard as he tried, he couldn't get the lid to close.

By the time Rex found the hiders, the lunch box was completely full.

"Hey, no fair!" Rex exclaimed. "I found you guys, but there's no room for me to hide with you. What do I do now, Woody?"

"Shhhh!" Woody said, raising a finger to his lips. "Keep your voice down or everyone will come over and see where we're hiding."

But it was too late. The rest of the toys were already hurrying towards the overstuffed lunch box.

"Oh, well," said Woody with a laugh. "They've found us, so this game is over. Everybody out!"

One by one, the toys tumbled out of the lunch box and gathered around Hamm.

"Gosh, Hamm, couldn't you have picked a bigger hiding place?" Rex asked.

Hamm replied, "Well, yeah, but isn't the point of the game to get squished? Like sardines in a can? The game is called 'sardines,' isn't it?"

The toys thought that over and had to agree. From then on, every time the toys played 'sardines,' the hider made sure to pick a small hiding place – just to keep things interesting!

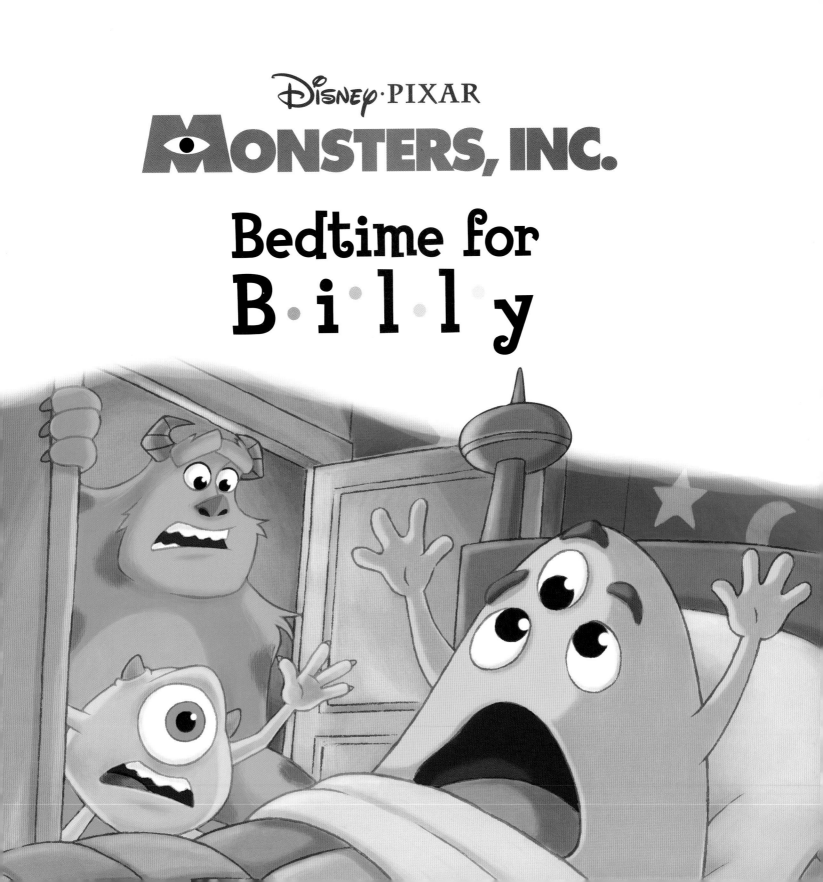

Mike the one-eyed monster and his best friend, Sulley, were excited about their evening. They were monster-sitting for Mike's nephew, Billy.

"Now, you be good," Billy's mother told her son.

"Don't worry, Mom, I will," he replied.

"Everything will be fine, Sis," said Mike proudly. "Sulley and I will take good care of the little guy. You don't have to worry about a thing."

"That's right," Sulley agreed.

Billy's parents kissed him good-bye and hopped in the car. His mum turned around and waved as they drove away.

The three monsters went inside and got some snacks ready. Then they ate pizza and popcorn while they watched classic movies like *Night of the Living Kids* and *Gross Encounters of the Kid Kind.*

After the movies were over, Mike and Sulley played Monster Boxing with Billy. Later, the three monsters listened to music, sang and danced. Billy and Mike even had a video-game contest!

The night flew by and soon it was bedtime.

"It's time for some shut-eye, Buddy," said Mike with a yawn. "Let's get you to bed!"

But putting Billy to bed wasn't going to be that easy. There was one very important detail that Billy's mother had forgotten to tell her monster-sitters.

Billy was scared of the dark!

"Aaaaaaahhhhh!!!!" screamed Billy.

"Wh-wh-what is it?" shouted Mike as he and Sulley ran back into the bedroom.

"There's a kid hiding in the c-closet . . ." stammered Billy. "It wants to g-get me!"

Mike and Sulley searched for human children. They checked the whole room, once with the lights on and twice with the lights off.

"There aren't any kids in the closet," said Mike.

"All clear under the bed," announced Sulley.

"See, there's nothing to worry about," Mike said. "You can go to sleep now."

But Billy was still frightened. Mike and Sulley quickly realized they had to come up with another plan to help him get over his fear.

They thought and thought. How could they show Billy that children weren't scary?

"I've got it!" exclaimed Mike. "The scrapbook!"

"You're a genius, Mikey!" declared Sulley.

Sulley and Mike hopped onto the bed next to Billy and the three monsters looked through the scrapbook. It was filled with photographs of monsters with children, newspaper clippings of them together and laugh reports.

"See, Billy," said Mike. "Human kids are not dangerous, and they love to have fun just like you."

"And they help us!" added Sulley. "Their laughter powers our city!"

"You know, Billy, sometimes human kids get scared of *us*," said Mike. "But once they see that we're funny and friendly, they realize there's no reason to be scared of monsters."

47

"This scrapbook shows that there's no reason to be afraid of human kids," added Sulley. "But just in case you get scared again, you can look through it to make yourself feel better."

Billy fell fast asleep as Mike and Sulley watched from the doorway.

"Another job well done, Mike," said Sulley.

"We're still the best team in the biz," replied Mike.

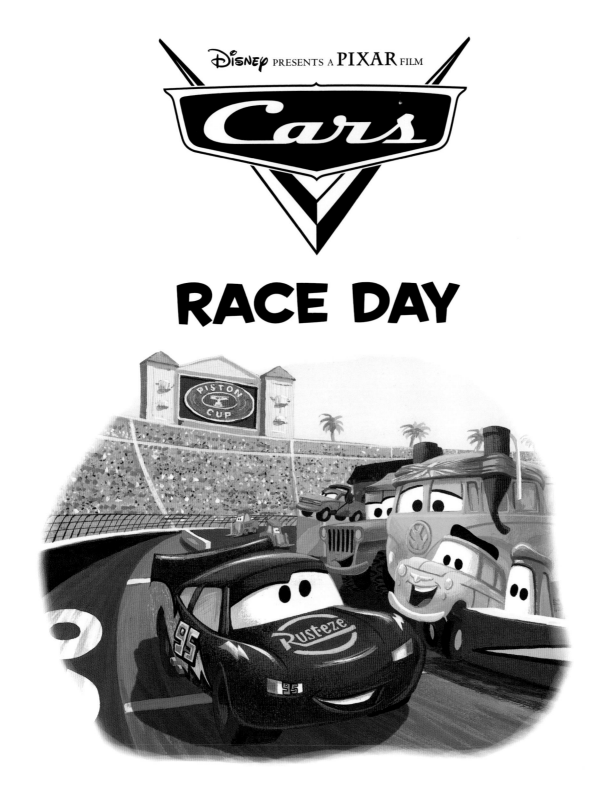

DISNEP PRESENTS A **PIXAR** FILM

Cars

RACE DAY

Vroom! Vroom! Three cars zoomed around the track at the Los Angeles International Speedway. They had just started the year's biggest race: the tiebreaker for the Piston Cup championship.

The race cars were in a dead heat. There was The King, a racing legend who was looking for one more win before retirement; Chick Hicks, a tough racer who had spent his career chasing The King's tailpipe; and Lightning McQueen, the rookie sensation who had taken the racing world by storm.

Just a week ago, all three race cars had tied for first place at the Dinoco 400 – a racing first. Today's tiebreaker would determine the winner once and for all.

A lot had happened to McQueen since the Dinoco 400. In fact, he wasn't really the same race car he once had been. On the way to California, he'd had a road mishap and had ended up in Radiator Springs, a remote, sleepy town. All the cars he'd met there had changed him – a lot.

At first, McQueen hated being stuck in the tiny town. He'd been separated from his driver, Mack and barreled into Radiator Springs in a panic. He'd sped out of control and crashed into everything, ruining the main road.

The town had sentenced McQueen to fix the pavement before he could leave. McQueen had wanted to go to his race, but the longer he'd stayed in Radiator Springs, the more he got to know the cars who lived there. And a funny thing happened – he began to like the little town.

A rusty tow truck named Mater became his best friend. He'd taught McQueen to drive backwards and to tip tractors. Sally was a blue sports car who'd taught him that the journey itself was sometimes more important than how quickly you got there. The race car had even got new tyres from Luigi and a sleek paint job from Ramone, two other cars from town.

When the press had found McQueen, he'd been hustled into a trailer to go to the big race. He hadn't really known how to say good-bye to his new friends.

Now, the cars were fifty laps into the race. The King had a short lead, with Chick Hicks and McQueen close behind. McQueen tried to pass Chick, but Chick squeezed him out.

McQueen tried to focus on the race, but his mind drifted off. He was thinking about the wonderful drive he'd had with Sally back in Radiator Springs.

As the rookie snapped out of his daydream, he realized he was heading into the wall. He gasped and braked hard, which made him spin into the infield.

McQueen just sat there, stunned, unable to move. The other two racers were already far ahead of him. The rookie wondered if he should even keep going. The race just didn't seem as important to him any more.

Just then, his radio crackled. "I didn't come here to see you quit," a familiar voice said. It was Doc!

McQueen looked over to his pit and saw Doc, along with a bunch of his friends from Radiator Springs: Sarge, Fillmore, Flo, Ramone, Sheriff, Guido and Luigi. He rolled into pit row.

"Guys!" McQueen called as he entered his pit. "You're here!" The race car was so excited, he could hardly contain himself.

"It was Doc's idea," said Ramone.

McQueen looked up at the crew-chief platform. The Radiator Springs town judge and doctor, Doc Hudson, was there, wearing his Fabulous Hudson Hornet logo, just like in his glory days.

After winning three Piston Cups, Doc had become a wreck. By the time he'd been fixed up, no one cared about him any more. He'd vowed never to return to the racing circuit. At first, he hadn't taken very kindly to McQueen, but the rookie's time in Radiator Springs had taught Doc a few things, too. Now here he was, supporting McQueen.

56

"I knew you needed a crew chief," Doc said
to McQueen. "But I didn't know it was this bad."

"Doc, look at you!" exclaimed McQueen. "I thought you said you'd never come back."

"I really didn't have a choice," replied Doc. "Mater didn't get to say good-bye."

McQueen looked over at the rusty, old tow truck, who grinned at him. The race car was glad to see his friend.

"All right," said Doc, getting McQueen's attention back, "if you can drive as good as you can fix a road, then you can win this race with your eyes shut. Now get back out there!"

McQueen revved his engine and sped onto the track. There was no way he was going to lose this race now!

"We are back in business!" Doc hooted over the radio.

McQueen was a lap behind. He drove hard and began making up ground quickly. With only sixty laps to go, McQueen caught up to the leaders. Chick saw that the rookie was trying to pass him.

As McQueen tried to make a move, Chick slammed into him.

The crash sent McQueen into a one-hundred and eighty-degree spin . . . but he kept on going and passed Chick while driving backwards. The crowd loved it. "I taught him that!" Mater said proudly.

McQueen gave Chick a quick smile and spun back around.

Fifty laps later, it was a dead heat. Chick pushed hard and tried to overtake McQueen. Now neck and neck, they bumped into each other. Suddenly, McQueen's tyres went flat.

Rubber and debris littered the raceway. McQueen headed for the pit. He had to get back out on the track before the pace car let The King and Chick go, or he'd be behind a lap. Guido changed the tyres quickly and McQueen pulled out just ahead of the pace car. He still had some ground to make up.

A few laps later, McQueen had caught up. Then the white flag dropped. This was it – the final lap. McQueen approached Chick and The King, ready to make his move.

McQueen went high around a turn. Chick tried to smash him against the wall. McQueen was sent spinning into the infield, but using a trick he had learned from Doc – turn right to go left – he recovered and took the lead, even passing The King. He was about to become the Piston Cup champion!

But Chick wasn't about to come in third. He rammed against The King. The racing veteran crashed into the wall and spun into the infield. The crowd gasped.

61

McQueen looked at the giant TV screen and saw what had happened to The King. He couldn't believe it. It reminded him of Doc's crash.

The rookie screeched to a stop just before crossing the finish line. He couldn't win, not like this. It just wasn't right.

Chick zoomed past him to win the race, but McQueen didn't care. He turned around and drove over to The King. The guy was a legend and McQueen didn't want to see him end his career like this.

"What are you doing, kid?" The King asked.

"I think The King should finish his last race," McQueen answered. He drove behind the battered race car and began pushing him forwards.

Everyone watched as the rookie edged The King over the finish line. The crowd went wild!

Chick celebrated his victory, but the crowd booed him off of the stage. No one cared that he had won the race because McQueen had won their hearts.

Meanwhile, McQueen pushed The King over to his crew. Then the rookie headed over to his own tent, where his friends were all waiting to congratulate him. Even Tex, Dinoco's owner and the biggest sponsor of the Piston Cup, wanted to talk to him.

"Hey, Lightning," Tex said to him, "how would you like to be the new face of Dinoco?"

"But I didn't win," McQueen replied.

"There's a whole lot more to racin' than just winnin'," said Tex.

McQueen was flattered, but as he looked back at his tent, he decided to stick with Rust-eze, the small company that had sponsored him all along.

But he did ask Tex for a favour . . . .

"Woo-hoo!" Mater cried. "Look at me – I'm flying!" It was two days after the race and the tow truck was soaring over Radiator Springs in the Dinoco helicopter. The race car had once promised his best friend a helicopter ride and he kept his promise.

Just then, McQueen drove up to his friend Sally.

"Just passing through?" she asked.

"You haven't heard?" he answered. "Yeah, there's a rumour floating around that some hotshot Piston Cup race car is setting up his big racing headquarters here."

She smiled, and they sped away together. McQueen had found a home. He was finally happy – even though he hadn't won the big race.

THE INCREDIBLES

A Super SUMMER BARBECUE

Disney PRESENTS A PIXAR FILM

One hot summer afternoon, Helen Parr stood in the kitchen frosting a chocolate cake. Her daughter, Violet, lay on the couch reading a magazine. Jack-Jack, the baby, sat in his high chair eating.

"Dash!" Helen called to her other son. "It's almost time to leave for the barbecue."

"Hey, Mum," complained Dash, running into the room at Super speed, "why do we have to go to some silly neighbourhood barbecue?"

"Dashiell Robert Parr," said Helen, "we're lucky to have been invited. It's our first neighbourhood party. You know we're doing our best to fit in here. And remember: *no* Super powers outside the house."

"Right, Mum. No Super powers. The barbecue should be *loads* of fun," said Dash, rolling his eyes.

Just then, Jack-Jack threw a bowl of mashed peas. In a flash, Helen stretched her arm across the kitchen and caught the bowl in midair. Helen's Super powers as Elastigirl could come in pretty handy around the house, but she knew if her family's powers were ever discovered, they would have to move again.

Bob Parr walked in through the front door. "Honey, I've got the lawn looking shipshape," he said as he flexed his muscles. Bob used to fight crime on a daily basis as the Super, Mr Incredible, but now his biggest weekend battle was the crabgrass.

He sighed. "I finally got the last of that giant tree stump. If I could have used my Super strength, I would've been done three hours ago."

"You're right, dear," Helen answered, giving him a kiss on the cheek. "But you know we have to do our best to behave like a normal family. I only have a few more boxes to unpack and I *don't* want to move this family again."

"No one will ever believe Violet is normal," said Dash.

Violet jumped up from the couch. "You be quiet!" she shouted. Then she threw a force field in Dash's path, knocking him to the ground.

"Kids, kids! That's enough. Let's get ready to go," said Helen.

A while later, the Parrs walked around the block to their first neighbourhood barbecue. Helen smiled at Jack-Jack, who was in a baby backpack. "I hope they like my cake," she said as she walked to the dessert table.

Bob headed over to the grill to help out. Violet looked around for someone to talk to.

Dash watched some children compete in a sack race. He couldn't race because it might reveal his Super speed.

Then a boy walked up to Dash. "Are you too chicken to play? *Bawk-bawk-bawk*," clucked the boy, flapping his arms. Some of the other children laughed.

Dash scowled. If only I could race, I'd show him – he thought. When the mean boy hopped by, he mysteriously tripped and fell.

"Weird," the boy said. "It felt like someone tripped me."

Dash smiled to himself and brushed off his sneaker. His speed had come in handy, after all. Luckily, his mum hadn't seen him.

Meanwhile, Helen was getting to know some other mothers and toddlers. She listened carefully as another woman talked about removing grass stains. When the woman began to discuss needlepoint, Helen realized that Jack-Jack had crawled away.

Out of the corner of her eye, Helen saw Jack-Jack atop a high brick wall. He was about to topple off! In a flash, Helen shot her

arm all the way across the yard and caught him. She sighed with relief and hugged Jack-Jack close to her. The other mother just rubbed her eyes and mumbled something about not sleeping much the night before. Oops, Helen thought to herself.

Over by the grill, the men talked about the previous night's baseball game. When the steak was ready, Bob stepped forwards. "Allow me," he said, as he picked up a knife. This steak is a bit tough, he thought. I'll just cut a little harder.

Craaack! All of a sudden, the table splintered in two. The meat went flying and landed in the dirt. Guess I used a little too much Super strength, Bob thought.

"They just don't make tables like they used to, do they fellas?" Bob asked, as the others laughed politely.

Violet hadn't found anyone her age, so she sat under a shady tree and began to read. Then an old lady came over. Violet stood up to introduce herself. Once she did, the woman wouldn't stop talking. She told Violet about her miniature duck collection, her dentures and even her hot-water bottle.

Finally, Violet couldn't stand it anymore. As the woman reached step thirty-three of her potato salad recipe, Violet pointed at something.

The woman turned and Violet seized the moment. She jumped behind a tall plant and used her Super powers to make herself invisible. Even though only her body disappeared, the colours of her clothes blended in with the bushes.

Minutes went by. Finally, the lady noticed that Violet wasn't standing next to her. She looked all around her and then walked away. When the coast was clear, Violet reappeared. She smiled to herself as she sat back down and opened her book.

Since the steak had fallen on the ground, Bob and the other guys decided to grill some hot dogs and hamburgers. Bob didn't help this time, but he did eat one or two more hot dogs than he should have.

Helen couldn't have been more pleased to see the neighbours enjoying her chocolate cake. Someone even asked for the recipe. She looked around the yard and spotted Dash telling a story. Violet was eating an ice cream cone with a girl her age.

Wow, it looks like we really fit in here, Helen thought as Bob walked over to her. He was finishing another hot dog.

Just then, she overheard one of the neighbours. "There's something strange about those Parrs," he said.

Helen grabbed Bob's arm. Bob looked at her. Had someone discovered them? Were their Super powers about to be revealed?

"Yeah, you should see how Bob mangled the table – and the steak!" a second neighbour said.

"Grandma said that Violet acted like she'd never heard of potato salad," a third neighbour chimed in. "And my son said Dash just *watched* the other kids race."

"All that may be true," someone else added, "but that Helen sure makes a terrific chocolate cake!" Everyone agreed, and the conversation ended.

The Parrs sighed with relief and chuckled to themselves. Their cover wasn't blown after all!

Maybe they were a little strange compared to the average family, but they were doing their best to act normal. Bob and Helen rounded up their children and headed for home, pleased with the way things had gone.

"I think we could really like this neighbourhood, Bob," said Helen, as they reached their house. Then she gave him a great big kiss, which the kids did their best to ignore.

"I think you're right," answered Bob. "I've got a good feeling about things this time."

"Sweetie, would you mind moving the car over a bit?" asked Helen. "I need to get out of the garage to go grocery shopping tomorrow morning."

"Sure thing, honey," answered Bob. "I'll be right in."

Bob looked at the car sitting in the driveway. The street was quiet. It's too easy, he thought to himself. Besides, a guy's gotta work out every now and then. Bob picked up the car, balanced it on one finger and put it down on the other side of the driveway. Dusting off his hands, he turned around to find Rusty, a little neighbourhood boy, sitting on his tricycle with his mouth hanging open.

"Uh, have a good evening, Rusty," said Bob, giving him a little wave. Then he went inside and enjoyed the rest of the evening with his Super family.

NEMO AND THE TANK GANG

One day, a little clown fish named Nemo got into big
trouble. When his father, Marlin, wasn't looking, he swam
out into the open ocean on a dare. Marlin realized what Nemo
had done and yelled at him to come back. Suddenly, a scuba
diver grabbed Nemo and put him in a bag. "Dad? Daddy?"
Nemo called, hoping his father could save him. But another
diver swam up and took a picture of Marlin. The flash blinded
him for a minute. The divers quickly
took Nemo back to their boat
and left.

The next thing
Nemo knew, he was
being plunged into
some strange water.

The clown fish swam straight into some scary-looking Tiki
heads. He screamed and then – *bam!* – he hit a glass wall.

Nemo realized that he was in a fish tank, which was
nothing like the ocean. It had glass walls all around and was
located in a dentist's office in Sydney, Australia. Nemo had
never been so far away from home – or his father.

When the dentist peered in at him, Nemo was so startled
he bumped into a fake treasure chest, which popped open and
let out a stream of bubbles. A yellow tang fish swam over and
tried to push all the bubbles back inside the chest.

Nemo didn't know what to think. Fish didn't act like this
in the ocean.

Then, a starfish named Peach unstuck herself from the glass and waved hello. Still a little scared, the clown fish hid inside a miniature diver's helmet. Before long, a whole gang of fish appeared and introduced themselves. There was Bloat, a blowfish; Deb, a blue-and-white humbug fish; Gurgle, a royal gramma fish; Jacques, a tiny cleaner shrimp; and Bubbles, a yellow tang fish who was crazy about bubbles.

Nemo thought the fish seemed friendly. When they learned he was from the ocean, or the Big Blue as they liked to call it, they were amazed. Most of them had come from pet stores.

Soon, a pelican named Nigel came by. Gurgle introduced the pelican to Nemo and told him how the clown fish had been taken from the reef.

When the dentist spotted Nigel, he shooed the pelican out of the open window, knocking over a frame with a photo of a little girl in it. "This here's Darla," the dentist told his patient. "She's my niece – going to be eight this week." Then he looked over at Nemo. "She's going to be here Friday to pick you up."

"She's a fish killer," muttered Peach.

Nemo panicked. He wanted to get back to his dad. He darted around the tank, but got stuck in the intake tube. "Daddy! Help me!" he cried.

A Moorish idol fish named Gill appeared from behind a plastic skull. "You can get yourself out," he said. "Just concentrate."

Nemo explained that one of his fins was smaller than the other. He didn't think he could do it. Gill showed him his own severed fin and said, "Never stopped me." So, Nemo swam as hard as he could. Before long, he had freed himself!

That night, Jacques woke up Nemo and led him to the volcano in the centre of the tank. As they got closer, Nemo spotted the rest of the fish. He wondered what was going on.

"We want you in our club, kid," Peach explained.

"*If* you are able to swim through the Ring of Fire!" Bloat added dramatically. A wall of bubbles erupted from the volcano. The Tank Gang chanted Nemo's name, urging him on.

The little clown fish concentrated and quickly zoomed through the bubbles.

Gill smiled at him. "From this moment on, you will now be known as *Shark Bait*," he said.

"Shark Bait's one of us now," Gill continued. He paused. "Darla's coming in five days. So what are we gonna do?"

No one said anything.

Luckily, Gill had an escape plan. Nemo was the only one small enough to swim into the filter and jam it with a pebble. If he completed that dangerous task, the tank would get dirty. The dentist would have to put the fish in bags while he cleaned it. Once he did, the Tank Gang would roll their bags down the counter, out of the window, off the awning, across the street and into the freedom of the harbour.

"Let's do it," Nemo said. He was anxious to get home to his dad.

The next day, while the Tank Gang was waiting for the dentist to take a break, Gill told Nemo that he'd injured his fin during his first escape attempt. He'd been trying to jump in the toilet.

"The toilet?" Nemo asked.

"All drains lead to the ocean, kid," the Moorish idol fish replied.

When the dentist left, Nemo gathered his courage, swam hard into the filter and jammed it with a pebble. The filter blades stopped for a moment, but then the pebble slipped and the deadly blades started whirling  again. Even worse, Nemo was being sucked backwards towards the blades!

His quick-thinking friends rushed into action. They pushed a plant into the tube and pulled Nemo back to safety. Gill's escape plan was ruined. The Tank Gang was silent. The Moorish idol fish swam away, ashamed that he'd put the little clown fish's life in danger.

Not long after that, Nigel heard an interesting bit of gossip. It was about a clown fish who was looking for his son. The tiny fish had battled three sharks, escaped from a hungry anglerfish and even survived a school of jellyfish. Now he was travelling towards Sydney! A bunch of sea turtles had given him a ride, then told other ocean creatures about the clown fish's adventures. When Nigel heard the story, he was sure that the fish had to be Nemo's father. He flew to the dentist's office to tell Nemo.

At first, the little clown fish didn't believe Nigel's story. His father was too scared to swim in the open ocean. Travelling this far meant Marlin was being very brave. Now Nemo felt brave, too. He was determined to escape from the tank and find his father as quickly as possible.

In a flash, Nemo picked up a new pebble and jammed it into the filter. This time, the plan worked – soon the tank would get very dirty.

The next day, the tank was covered with green algae. Nemo knew there was a chance he might get to go home soon.

"Look at that," Gill said to Nemo. "Absolutely filthy. And it's all thanks to you, kid."

Nemo giggled. Then Gill caught Jacques cleaning and had to tell him to stop. Bloat, on the other hand, loved wallowing around in the muck.

When the dentist came in, he ran his finger along the inside of the tank. He sighed and told his receptionist he'd have to clean it before Darla arrived to pick up her new fish the next morning.

"Yay! He's going to clean the tank!" Nemo cried.

"Are you ready to see your dad, kid?" Gill asked.

"Uh-huh," Nemo said longingly.

But when the fish woke up the next morning, the tank was spotless. The dentist had installed a new filter during the night. The Tank Gang's escape plan had failed again. And Darla was due any minute!

The dentist soon arrived and scooped Nemo into a net. The little clown fish panicked and the Tank Gang reacted quickly. They scrambled into the net with him and swam downwards, forcing the dentist to drop them. The fish began to cheer, but the dentist snuck up behind Nemo and caught him in a plastic bag. Then he set the bag on the counter.

Gill and the others coached Nemo to roll the bag towards the window. He had almost made it there when the dentist noticed and moved him.

Just then, Darla came in. She was anxious to see her birthday surprise. Nemo knew that he would have to do something if he wanted to survive. So he floated belly up. The dentist looked at the little clown fish and thought he had died.

Nemo winked at the Tank Gang, sure the dentist was going to flush him down the toilet. Thanks to Gill, he knew the drain would take him to the ocean.

All of a sudden, Nigel flew in with Marlin and Dory, a fish who'd been helping with the search. Marlin saw Nemo and thought that he was dead. Nigel dropped the fish back into the ocean.

Darla began to shake the bag, so the Tank Gang catapulted Gill onto her head. She dropped the bag. It burst open and Nemo landed on a tray of tools. Gill helped him get to the spit sink.

Nemo went down the drain and soon made it to the ocean, where he found his father. They were thrilled to see each other again.

Before long, the Tank Gang broke the filter and were able to find their way to the Big Blue at last!

MIKE'S DOG PROBLEM

It was business as usual at the new Monsters, Inc., where monsters collected laughs from human children to use as energy.

Mike Wazowski was one of the top Laugh Collectors. He told funny jokes and made children giggle a lot. But lately, he was having trouble on the job.

"Oh, no, not again!" Mike groaned as he read the paperwork for his next assignment. "This kid has a dog!"

Mike was terrified of dogs, but no one else knew. He was too embarrassed to say anything.

I can't make kids laugh when there's a dog around, thought Mike.

Those drooling fur-bags think I'm a big rubber ball!

He really didn't want to face another dog. So he needed to come up with a good excuse to skip work.

He paced the Laugh Floor, trying to think of something. "I can say I have monster pox," he said to himself.

Just then, Mike's friend, Sulley, arrived on the Laugh Floor.

The big blue monster was the new president of Monsters, Inc.

"What are you waiting for, buddy?" asked Sulley. "There are kids to crack up and laughs to collect."

"I . . . uh . . . dropped my contact lens," said Mike.

"Good one, funnyman," said Sulley as he pushed Mike towards the door. "The kids will love your new material."

Reluctantly, Mike walked through the door into the boy's bedroom. He saw the dog and immediately jumped up on a stool to get as far from it as he could. He hoped that the dog would go away so that he could tell jokes in peace.

But this was a playful dog. It ran up to the stool and sat in front of Mike, who got so nervous, he couldn't remember his jokes. The boy didn't laugh at all. Mike was very upset. He would have to go back to work without any laughs.

When Mike hopped off of the stool, the dog jumped up so he could shake its paw.

"*Aaaaah!*" Mike screamed and held a stool between himself and the dog. He backed towards the closet. As he was shutting the door, he noticed that the boy sitting on the bed was frowning.

Mike was sad. Children usually loved it when he came to tell jokes. But he just couldn't relax when dogs were around.

The next day, Mike was assigned to the same room because he hadn't collected enough laughs. Sulley noticed that Mike didn't want to go. So he snuck in behind him to find out why.

Inside, Mike tried to tell a joke – but he was so nervous that he just froze with fear.

"Nice d-doggy, good d-doggy," he stuttered.

Suddenly, Sulley realized that his friend was afraid of dogs!

That day after work, Sulley asked Mike why he was scared around dogs.

"I feel like a giant chew toy when I'm near them, like any second they might bite me!" cried Mike.

"Don't worry, pal," Sulley said. "I'll show you some things to do when you're around dogs – and maybe you won't get as frightened next time you see one."

Sulley taught Mike all about dogs and gave him some safety tips. Together they read stories and watched videos about friendly dogs.

"Remember, Mike, even though dogs slobber, have big teeth, and make loud noises, that doesn't mean they're scary. We have a lot of loud, slobbering friends – just think of our pal Ricky."

Mike laughed. Maybe Sulley is right, he thought.

The next day, he and Sulley went to a room with a
dog. Mike remembered what Sulley had taught him –
to stay calm and let the dog sniff him. He took a deep
breath. The dog bounded over and sniffed Mike, who

tried to relax. He
looked over at
Sulley, who gave
him a thumb's
up. The dog was
friendly and Mike began
to feel comfortable. Soon
he was telling one joke
after another.

Thanks to Sulley's help, Mike became the top Laugh Collector again – and he even grew to like dogs.

"Maybe *I'll* get a dog," declared Mike.

"Maybe you should start with a hamster," Sulley said with a chuckle.

DISNEP PRESENTS A PIXAR FILM

THE INCREDIBLES

SUPER ANNOYING!

Dashiell Robert Parr was bored. It was Saturday afternoon and he had run out of things to do. He had already taken a twenty-mile run, cooled off with fifty laps at the town pool and chased the neighbour's dog around the block. But with his Super speed, that had only taken about five minutes.

Dash sat on his bed, wondering what to do. Just then, his mother, Helen, walked past.

"You know," she said as she looked around her son's messy room, "if you're looking for something to do, you could clean up your . . ." Before Helen had a chance to finish, Dash raced around his room and cleaned it up.

"I'm still bored," he said with a groan.

"Well, you could . . . work on your math homework," Helen said as she left his room.

Homework, now? Dash thought. I'll do that tomorrow instead. Right now I want to do something fun.

Brrrng! The telephone rang. Dash's sister, Violet, raced out of her bedroom to answer it.

Dash had spotted his target. "This will be fun," he said to himself. He stopped in Violet's doorway and grinned slyly.

Dash's eyes darted back and forth between Violet's bedroom and the kitchen. He wanted to make sure his sister wasn't looking. Then he hurried into her room.

Five minutes later, Violet returned to her room. She started to walk towards her bed, but halfway there she stopped in her tracks. Things were not as she had left them.

The bedspread was upside down. The shade on her lamp was missing; her books had been moved around; and the pictures that hung around her mirror were rearranged. Only one person would have done this.

"Mum!" Violet yelled. "Dash messed up my room. Nothing is where it's supposed to be."

As Helen walked down the hall, a breeze whipped through Violet's room. Helen looked inside. "It looks fine to me, honey. Your brother is doing his homework in his room. Now I've got to get dinner ready," she said.

She thinks my room looks fine? Violet wondered. It's a complete mess! She turned around and scanned the room. Everything was back in place. Then her eyes fell on the closet door, which was slightly ajar. She went over to the door and threw it open.

"Dash!" Violet exclaimed as she pushed some clothes aside. "Get out of here, you little insect!"

Dash jumped up wearing some of his sister's clothes. "Look at me. I'm Violet. I'm in love with Tony Rydinger."

Violet tried to pull him out of the closet, but he raced into the hall.

"Stay out of my room!" she yelled, slamming her door shut.

Dash dropped the clothes in the hall and sped out to the backyard. He stood on tiptoe and peered into his sister's bedroom window.

Violet hadn't even had time to cross the room and sit on her bed before she spotted her little brother.

"Yoo-hoo, Violet!" Dash called to her in a singsong voice as he threw her a dainty wave.

Violet rushed to the window and pulled down the blind.

Violet was glad she was finally rid of her annoying brother. But as she sat on her bed, she felt something under her. "*Aaaahhh!*" she screamed.

"Forget to lock something?" Dash said, poking his head out from under the covers. Then he zoomed around and around –

up onto the bed, down to the floor, around Violet – all at such Super speed that Violet couldn't tell where he was at any given moment. All she saw was a blur flying around her room, kicking up a whirlwind  of papers and blowing pictures off of her mirror.

"Dash!" Violet shouted. "Knock it off!"

But Dash only came to a halt when he spotted Violet's diary, which had fallen open on her bed.

"Ooooh," Dash said, picking up the diary and eyeing it excitedly. "What have we here? Oh . . . poetry." Dash continued in a fake English accent: "'I love Tony. He dost the cutest. Shall I compare him to a . . .'"

That was it. Violet had had enough of Dash. "Give that back!" she yelled.

Dash tried to race out of the room, but Violet threw a force field in front of the door. Dash ran into it head-on and was knocked to the floor. The diary fell out of his hand and Violet quickly snatched it away. But before she knew it, the diary flew out of her hand in a sudden wind.

"'How dost I love thee?'" Dash read from the other side of the room.

Violet turned invisible and lunged at Dash. "You are gonna get it!" she cried.

Dash and Violet continued to chase each other around Violet's room in a blur of Super powers.

A while later, they heard their mum calling to them. "Violet! Dash!" she cried. "Time for dinner!"

Dash froze. Then, in the blink of an eye, he zipped out through the bedroom door and down the hall to the kitchen table.

"Dash," Helen asked, "did you finish your homework?"

Then Violet appeared at the table. Her hair was all mussed.

"Nah," Dash replied with a smile. "I found something better to do."

DISNEY PRESENTS A PIXAR FILM

Cars

RED'S
TUNE-UP BLUES

One morning, Red the fire engine woke up. The sun was shining in through the fire station door. It's the perfect day to plant a new garden, Red thought as he started his engine.

Rrrrrr. Rrrr-urr-urr. Red's engine sounded funny. *Pop! Pop! Pop!* Now loud noises were coming out of his tailpipe.

As his engine sputtered, Red tried to shrug it off. Hopefully, whatever was wrong would go away, because Red did not want to go to Doc's clinic. He'd never been, but he sure didn't like the idea of being poked and prodded. Some of the tools Doc used were awfully loud. Just the thought of going upset Red's tank.

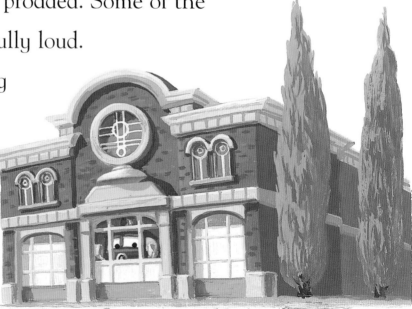

Red decided to go for a drive. Maybe that would make him feel better.

As he drove
out of town, Red
passed
Lightning
McQueen.

"Hey, Red!"
McQueen
greeted him.
"How's it going?"

"Fine," Red replied shyly. *Bang! Bang!*

"Whoa!" exclaimed McQueen. "That can't feel good.
You okay?"

"Mmm-hmm," said Red.

McQueen watched as Red drove away. He could hear that
Red's engine wasn't firing right. He's probably afraid to get it
checked out, thought McQueen.

127

A few minutes later, McQueen got an idea. If he could get Red to race him to the clinic, maybe he could trick him into going inside.

"Hey, Red!" McQueen shouted as he caught up to the fire engine, who was turning around. The little stretch of road that Red had already driven had made him feel worse, so he decided he would go back to town and work on the garden. Maybe that would help.

"You want to race into town?" McQueen asked him. "I'll give you a head start. What do you say?"

"Oh . . ." *Hic!* "No!" said Red, sputtering. "You're too fast."

"C'mon, Red. I'll even drive backward, just like Mater taught me," insisted McQueen. "It'll be fun."

"No, thanks," said Red. "Have to plant my flowers."

Pop! Red started driving towards town.

McQueen headed into town, too, to find his friends. They wouldn't want Red to be sick.

McQueen found everyone at Flo's V8 Café, filling up on breakfast.

"Good morning, *mi amigo*," Ramone greeted him. "Beautiful day, eh?"

"Yeah, it is," said McQueen, "except for one problem."

"What could that-a be?" asked Luigi, the tyre-shop owner.

"Red's not running right," McQueen explained as he pointed to the fire engine, who was starting to plant a garden across the street. "But he's afraid to go to the clinic."

"Aw, shucks," said Mater the tow truck. "I know how the poor fella feels. I was scared my first time, too! But Doc's a pro. He'll have Red fixed up before he knows what hit him!"

"We've got to get him there first," said McQueen.

"That silly boy," said Flo. "Let me see if I can talk to him."

Flo began to drive towards Red.

Even from a distance, Flo could hear Red's engine rumbling.

"Hey there, Red!" she called out. "You're sounding a little rough this morning. When was the last time you went in for a tune-up?"

"Oh, uh . . ."

"That's what I thought," said Flo. "Honey, you need to get yourself in there."

Red looked down nervously.

"How about," continued Flo, "you go get checked out. Then, afterward, come by the café for a free tank of my best fuel?"

"Gee, Flo," said Red. "Thanks, but I'm all right." The truck went back to his flowers.

"I tell you," Flo said to her friends when she returned to the V8, "that is one stubborn fire engine."

"Don't take it personally, baby," said Ramone, Flo's husband and the owner of Ramone's House of Body Art. "Let me try."

Ramone drove over to Red. "Hey, my friend, you look like you could use some brightening up."

"Hello, Ramone," said Red. "I'm fine."

"No, really, man," Ramone said. "It's today's paint-shop special – a new coat of paint and a custom flame job, free with a visit to Doc's. You'll be the hottest fire engine around."

"Thanks, Ramone . . . but no."

Red continued with his new flower bed. Ramone could see Red wasn't making much progress. So far, he hadn't even planted one flower!

Ramone returned to Flo's. "Couldn't talk him into it," he said.

"What that boy needs is some discipline," said Sarge, who had just driven in with his neighbour, Fillmore.

Sarge rolled over behind Red. "Hut two!" roared Sarge.

"Aaaaahh!" screamed Red.

"I order you to go to Doc's in the next five minutes and get yourself a thorough once-over!" Sarge demanded.

Red just looked at Sarge and shook his head.

"Don't you eyeball me!" yelled Sarge. "Get on the street and start rolling, soldier! Move it, move it, move it!"

Red looked down and began to cry.

From across the street at Flo's everyone could see that Sarge's method wasn't working.

"We had better get over there before Red drives away," McQueen said to Sally, who had just rolled up.

The two cars sped over. Mater, Luigi, Guido, Fillmore, Flo and Ramone followed.

"Okay, Sarge!" yelled McQueen. "That's enough."

"Show him a little love, man," said Fillmore.

"Oh, well, I tried," said Sarge. He turned to Red. "I didn't mean to scare you, Red. No hard feelings, I hope."

135

"It's okay," Red replied, swallowing a sob. After a minute, he stopped crying.

"Oh, it is so-a nice to see two friends make up-a," said Luigi. "I tell you what, Red, since you are my friend, too, I make-a you this-a promise. You go to the clinic, I give you new set of tyres. What you say?"

"Well," said Red thoughtfully, "my tyres are shabby. . . ."

Everyone waited. Was Red finally going to agree to go?

"But I don't think so," the fire truck finished.

Everyone groaned. They had been so close! It looked like they would have to come up with another idea.

Then Mater thought of something. "I'll take you tractor tipping!" the tow truck promised. "Once you knock over a tractor and hear it snort, you'll be laughing so hard, you'll forget you even went to Doc's."

"Thanks, Mater, but no," said Red. "And don't worry, friends, I'll be okay." Red turned away from the other cars and looked back down at his new flower bed. He sighed. He was so tired and he hadn't got very far.

Bang! Pop, pop, pop! Red's engine gurgled and more loud noises came out of his tailpipe.

"Dad gum!" said Mater. "I reckon that's about the worst sound I ever heard come out of you."

Sally decided it was time for one last try. She inched forwards.

"Listen, Red," said Sally. "We all know going to get a tune-up for the first time can be scary. But whatever is wrong could be easy to fix. If you don't go now, it could turn into a bigger problem later. None of us wants you to need a complete overhaul.

We care too much about you."

Red looked back at his friends. He knew what Sally said was true.

"Will you go with me?" he asked Sally.

"Of course I will," she replied.

"We'll all go," said McQueen. "We wouldn't let you go it alone, pal."

Red smiled.

Later that day, Red rolled out of the clinic. All his friends were waiting for him.

"That wasn't so bad," he told them. "I feel great."

Doc followed Red. "He's all fixed up, guys and healthy as a horse!" Doc proclaimed.

"All right, Red!" said McQueen. "How about that race?"

"Okay," said Red, "and then I'll plant my flowers."

"You go ahead," said McQueen. "I'll be ready when you are."

Red revved his engine. *Vroom!* It sounded smooth as silk. He took off.

As McQueen started to catch up, Red turned his siren on full blast. *Wooooo-woooooo.*

McQueen was so startled that he veered off of the road into the bushes. Sally, Doc and the other cars giggled. Red smiled and sped forwards. It was good to be running on all cylinders

Buzz to the Rescue!

"There you go, pardners," Andy said as he packed Sheriff Woody, Jessie the cowgirl and Bullseye the horse into his backpack. He was taking them to Cowboy Camp and Jessie couldn't wait. Woody had told her there were *real* horses there.

"Almost ready?" Andy's mum asked as she poked her head into his room. Glancing at the half-open backpack, she shook her head. "You know the rules. You can only take one toy to camp with you."

"Oh, all right," Andy said with a sigh. "Sorry, guys." He lifted Jessie and Bullseye out of the bag and placed them on the windowsill.

The two toys watched from the window as Andy walked to the car. Bullseye nuzzled Jessie's shoulder and she patted him on the head.

"I'm disappointed, too," she said sadly.

Bullseye whinnied as Jessie climbed down from the window and flopped into a box full of books. Andy's mum had just put the box in his room that morning and Jessie thought its high sides would make a nice place to sit by herself. She had only been there a moment when Buzz Lightyear, a space ranger, poked his head over the side of the box.

"Don't be sad, Jessie," Buzz said, climbing into the box. "You don't need to go to camp to have an adventure. We can have a great time here. Right, guys?"

All of Andy's toys agreed. Rex the dinosaur, Hamm the piggy bank, and Slinky Dog gathered around to cheer up Jessie. Buzz jumped out of the box to lead everyone on an adventure.

Suddenly, a Green Army Man yelled, "Red alert!"

Someone was coming. All of the toys fell lifelessly to the floor as the doorknob turned. Jessie was still inside the box.

The babysitter for Andy's little sister walked in. She looked at the list Andy's mother had given her. "Let's see . . . 'Put box of old books in attic,'" she read.

Old books, Jessie thought. Oh, no! While the babysitter peered at the list, Jessie glanced down at the side of the box. It read: OLD BOOKS.

The babysitter picked up the box Jessie was in and took it to the attic. As soon as she had left Andy's bedroom, the rest of the toys looked at each other in shock.

"We've got to do something!" Buzz cried. "Gather 'round, everybody!"

Jessie lay perfectly still as the babysitter turned out the light and closed the attic door. When she was gone, the cowgirl climbed out of the box and ran to the door.

She pushed and pulled on the door, but it would not budge. Looking around the attic, Jessie spotted a small window. She climbed up on a few boxes so she could look out.

The view was exactly the same as the one from Andy's window – only higher. Jessie realized that Andy's room must be directly below. Suddenly, she had an idea. She began to look around for some rope.

147

Meanwhile, Buzz and the other toys were planning a rescue.

"Okay, recruits, here's the plan," Buzz said as he pointed to Etch A Sketch, who quickly drew a picture of the stairs to the attic.

"The Green Army Men will lead the attack and radio back if they run into danger," Buzz explained. "At the top of the stairs, they will form a pyramid, grab onto the doorknob and open the door." Etch A Sketch drew the plan as Buzz spoke. "Once the door is open, I'll go in and get Jessie," the space ranger added. "The rest of you should stand watch at the bottom of the steps."

The toys nodded. They all knew what to do.

"Let's go, everyone!" Buzz cried. "We've got a toy to save!"

With that, the toys headed upstairs.

Up in the attic, Jessie managed to open an old trunk and hop inside. She looked around and found some old newspapers, three books, a baby blanket and – a jump rope!

Jessie pulled the jump rope out of the trunk and tied it into a quick slipknot. "It's not the best lasso I've ever seen," she said to herself, "but it'll have to do."

She twirled the makeshift lasso a few times and threw the loop over the window lock. Next, she hauled herself up onto the ledge. She opened the window a few inches and crawled outside.

"Don't look down," she told herself as she stepped onto the ledge.

Just then, Jessie heard someone fiddling with the attic doorknob. Oh, no, she thought. The babysitter is back! Jessie closed her eyes, grabbed the rope and jumped.

But the noise outside the door wasn't the babysitter at all. It was the other toys and they were just about ready to enter the attic and rescue Jessie.

"Green Army Men, fall in!" Sarge commanded.

He turned to Buzz and gave him a snappy salute. Then he faced his men and barked a few commands. Within moments, they had formed a pyramid.

Buzz held his breath as the Green Army Man at the top grabbed the knob. He fumbled with it, but after a moment it turned – the door was open!

"Hang on, Jessie!" Buzz cried as he ran into the attic. "We'll rescue you!"

But Jessie was nowhere to be found!

Buzz looked around. He gasped when he spotted the open window. Scrambling up some old cardboard boxes, Buzz climbed onto the outside ledge. Looking down, he saw Jessie hanging onto a jump rope.

"Don't let go, Jessie!" Buzz shouted. "I'm coming for you!"

Buzz deployed his wings. Then, taking a deep breath, he dove out the window.

Jessie looked up and saw Buzz falling out the attic window – right towards her. He was trying to rescue her – he didn't know she was climbing down the rope.

"Look out!" Buzz cried.

Thinking fast, Jessie swung her legs out and caught Buzz just as he was about to fall past her. He was heavy and the rope jerked under his weight.

"Whoa!" Jessie shouted as they swung forwards – right through Andy's open window.

The rest of the toys raced down the stairs to Andy's room. Buzz and Jessie were lying on the floor.

"Are you okay?" Rex asked.

Buzz was the first to sit up. "I'm more than okay!" he crowed. "Our rescue effort was successful, everyone! We saved Jessie!"

Jessie laughed and stood up. "Saved me?" She paused. I was the one who rescued Buzz, she thought. What does it matter, though? The other toys looked at her.

"Well, thanks, everybody!" Jessie grinned as she looked around at her friends. "Even though I didn't get to go to Cowboy Camp, this has been the best adventure ever! Yee-hah!"

"Yee-hah!" all the toys cheered.

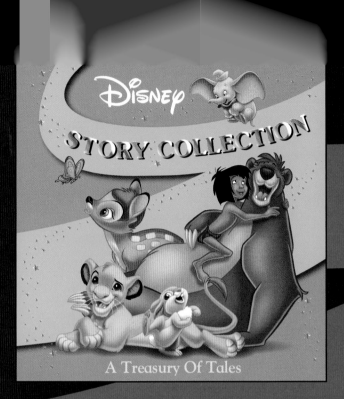

Disney
STORY COLLECTION
A Treasury Of Tales

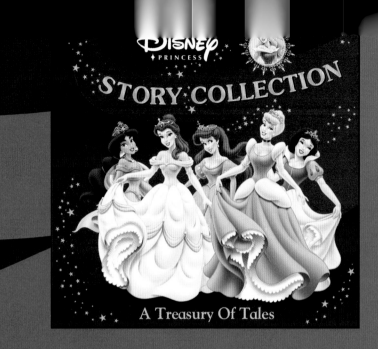

DISNEY
PRINCESS
STORY COLLECTION
A Treasury Of Tales

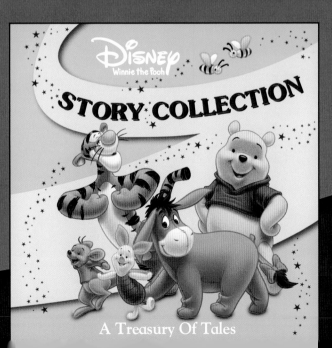

Disney
Winnie the Pooh
STORY COLLECTION
A Treasury Of Tales